My Autistic Filter:

An inside look at how one autistic person processes information

Zarqnon the Embarrassed

Dedicated

To Mom and Dad,
>who gave me the tools to survive long before I understood what was going on,

To Matthew and Jonathan,
>who inspire me every day,

And most of all, to my beautiful Hope,
>who has walked with me through this journey of discovery. You are so beautiful to me!

De Coloures

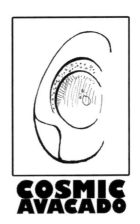

Edition 1 © 2019 Zarqnon

ISBN-13: 978-1703605426 (Custom Universal)

INTRO

Autism was first called "autism" in the late 1930s. Although the word was used then, the condition was still viewed as an extension of other neuro-conditions. It wasn't until some 30ish years later that it was even considered its own unique characteristic. Today, autism is still being redefined and studied to understand its causes, how it functions, and where the boundaries of "who is and who is not" lay.

WHO I AM

My name is Joseph McLaughlin. I use imaginative pseudonyms because I enjoy creating and naming characters. I am not trying to be silly or hide things. I just enjoy it, and one of the things I have learned over the years is to embrace the things I enjoy.

I was born with hydrocephalus (water on the brain), and I have had too many surgeries to count. Most of my peculiarities my entire life have been chalked up to the hydrocephalus. It is said that the apple doesn't fall too from the tree. When the apples acted just like the tree, it became apparent that I shared more than genes with my boys. My actions and struggles suddenly seemed a lot less related to the hydrocephalus that I suffered from all my life. Hydrocephalus can cause brain injuries, but those injuries are not genetic or transferable from one generation to the next. It turns out that autism runs in families, and I apparently had passed along something I didn't even know I had, but had been affecting me my entire life. When I had children and they were diagnosed with autism, so much of my life began to make sense.

This is common - especially with older people who may be on the spectrum. Since the autism spectrum was a vague concept that carried a lot of stigmas when I was born (60s), and most people my age had our peculiarities chalked up to bad parenting, illness, injury, anger issues, and so forth. In my case, the hydrocephalus made a good scapegoat. I didn't have to be lumped in with the "misbehaving" children. I was just "sick".

I learned I was autistic when I was almost 40 (when the apple was diagnosed). Everything changed in how I interpreted my "peculiarities". When people ask if it is important for their child to be diagnosed or are afraid of labels, I simply tell them the most important thing for the child or adult is to know why they function the way they do. We KNOW we are different. We don't need a doctor/psychiatrist/life coach to tell us that. We know it. But if we don't know why, we spend a lot of time trying to develop coping mechanisms - many of which are unhealthy.

My past is littered with train wrecks: failed relationships, mountains of debt, and trashed careers. I offended countless people without realizing it.—all because I had no clue how my brain was interpreting the world around me, or how the world around me was filtering my behaviors.

I want to share my failures with you so I can also share with you the other side of the mountain in the hopes someone who is struggling may hear a familiar voice, and then see that there is hope just beyond the horizon.

Filters

Our brains are pounded with billions of signals every day, from touch, sound, sight, and so forth. Those signals can be grand, like listening to a concert, or they can be very subdued, like barometric pressure and the sound of air conditioners. Understanding how brains filter information is one of the key distinctions between how autistic individuals and "neuro-typical" individuals interpret data.

And then, after we interpret the data, we may have many different ways to respond, including speech, clapping, making a decision, taking naps, eating a snack, wrapping up, and so forth.

People like me have filters that are suppressed and do not allocate signals properly.

The brain uses filters:

- to send "eye signals" to the "eye center" of the brain
- to send words to the mouth
- to catch a ball
- to "filter facial clues" to interpret individuals
- to organize time
- to zero in on who is talking to us
- to determine the difference between proper and improper
- to organize thought and learning processes to specific topics
- to derive lists

If filters are compromised (deviated, broken, overloaded), then these functions may be affected: signals may not make it to where they are supposed to go, and/or they may make it to more places than they were supposed to go.

Without these filters, it can make many of these things listed difficult/almost impossible. On the other hand, the absence, deviation, or suppression of those filters can allow the individual to see things in a light that others cannot.

UNDERSTANDING HOW THE DIFFERENT FILTERS WORK

When you see pictures comparing brain scans between autistic and non-autistic individuals, this is the typical gist you will see: one image represent a non-autistic individual showing signals going from the filter (in the front of the brain) to the location of the brain that processes those specific signals.

This next image is of the autistic person under the same stimuli, where the signal leaves the filtering area and overflows the brain. The signals received go haphazardly through the brain and may or may not hit the proper processing unit of the brain. The number of signals that do make it is not equivalent to the signals firing correctly in the non-autistic counterpart.

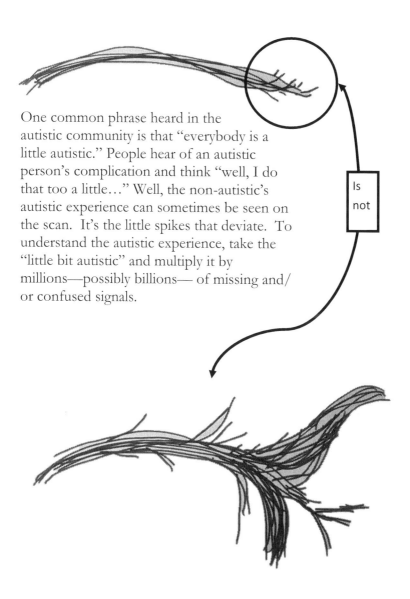

One common phrase heard in the autistic community is that "everybody is a little autistic." People hear of an autistic person's complication and think "well, I do that too a little…" Well, the non-autistic's autistic experience can sometimes be seen on the scan. It's the little spikes that deviate. To understand the autistic experience, take the "little bit autistic" and multiply it by millions—possibly billions— of missing and/or confused signals.

Is not

SYSTEMATIC PROCEDURE

A healthy filtering system allows knowledge to build upon the information as it is received. The secondary information can connect to the primary information, the tertiary information connects to the secondary information, etc…

For example: in vocabulary, math or science, we learn the first concept. After that, we go to the second concept, which builds on the first. Then we go to the third concept that builds on the second.

In short, neuro-typical brains learn A, then B, then C…

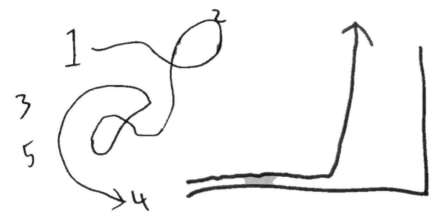

I cannot stack information on top of the next because I cannot filter out the correct piece of information to stack. Instead, I absorb all the information. When all the pieces eventually fall together in my head, it appears as if I went from 0 to infinity overnight. After the processing lag, my brain is able to take all the information and develop a concept that I can integrate into my intuitive knowledge base. I don't have to filter and stack, I see the topic in a holistic manner.

For example: I learn a concept, and I dump it in a bucket. I learn another concept and I dump it in a bucket. I learn a third concept and I dump it in the bucket. I swirl it around and look for something that makes sense. Once I find something that makes sense, I pull it out and rapidly start attaching everything else to it. Sometimes the way it is pulled out resembles typical results. But more often than not, the pieces are rearranged in a very non-conventional fashion.

Note that the original three concepts don't have to be necessarily relational or systematically related. I still find some way to connect them in the bucket. This is one of the ways people on the spectrum come up with "crazy/ingenious" ideas— people like me dump a lot of seemingly non-corollary items in the bucket and look for connections.

In short: throw all the letters in a bowl and then all the bowls in a bucket, shake it up and look for neat words...

PROCEDURE VS EXPERIMENTATION

Without those filters, people like me become "highly experimental", pinging off walls and floors and ceilings in exploring a concept or developing new skills. I don't simply filter a topic and slowly build on it. I am dipping back into the pond constantly and experimenting until the concept solidifies somewhere in our head. I am sticking the Lego on the Barbie to calculate the circumference of a watermelon.

Literally, I go "I think it works this way"…I run into a wall - WHAM!
"OK, maybe it works this way"… another wall—WHAM!
"OK, maybe it works this way"…WHAM! WHAM!

In short: WHAM! WHAM! WHAM! WHAM!

Following the Topic

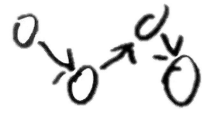

The ability to stack information empowers the working memory to be able to stack and organize information into a usable, on the fly, tool.

We can take those procedures to stick on topic, develop plans of action, and remember steps to obtain a goal. If we are given a list, we can organize it. If we are given a series of thoughts, we can organize them in a functional procedure to carry it out.

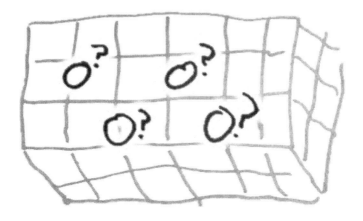

Without the filter, short term/ working memory like mine is limited because the ability to organize incoming information is reduced. There is no intuitive connection between steps. I have difficulty memorizing lists over 2 items. If someone is giving me several instructions, I am already forgetting them by the third instruction.

Systematic

To wrap up the previous illustrations, the filters allow the brain to focus and organize data so that information can be organized and built upon. The filter can also be used to process on the go data and make on the fly decisions.

UNIQUE

Without those filters, my brain has a reduced ability to use a systematic process in aggregating data. On the same line, processing data on the fly is limited since my brain cannot filter data into usable information spontaneously. Instead, data is pooled and unceremoniously accrued on a loosely interwoven matrix which is accessed in a haphazard fashion.

If I answer quickly, it is because the data is swimming at the top of the pool.

LOOKING AND LISTENING

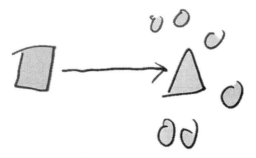

In a typical design, the brain knows how to filter out visual and auditory noise to focus on what an individual is looking at or listening to. The brain can filter out a person standing in a crowd, or hear a person speaking to them in a room full of people. If something or someone interrupts or interferes, it is a "distraction". The brain literally filters out other sounds or visuals.

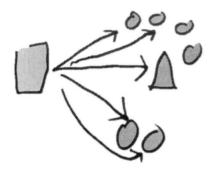

My brain is actively engaged with every object, every voice, everything: air conditioners, tvs, moving objects, other conversations… These things are not interrupting or are distractions: My brain is literally having a conversation with these things simultaneously.

Sometimes words are used like "He has zoned out, he doesn't hear anything," when actually I am hearing everything all at once. Everything. Your words. The air conditioner. The TV. The florescent lights. People walking by. Everything. And I am remembering what was said. And forty plus years later, I still remember what was said.

Likewise, while a non-autistic person can usually visually filter out everything around the person they are focusing on, a person like me cannot. I see a whole picture. And I have to consciously pull the person out of the picture. When I am "looking for my wife in a crowd," my wife waves her hand, even when she is right in front of me. All I see is a cloud of people and it is very difficult for me to pull her out of it.

THE 5 SENSES

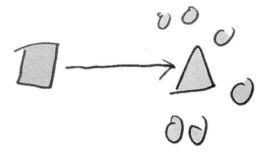

People who have good filters typically have direct correlation between their senses and their sensory processors. When they see something, the signal goes <u>directly to</u> and <u>only to</u> the vital section of the brain that processes sight. When they experience touch, the brain responds to it <u>as touch</u> and interprets the level and class of touch (friendly, danger, agitation, etc)

In short: the eye stuff goes to the eye part of the brain. The hearing stuff goes to the hearing part of the brain.

This doesn't include "trained responses", like if we see a hand get hit, we feel it being hit, or specific "painful noises". These are actually "filtered responses" as well, in that the brain is rewired to directly react to sensory stimuli. The filtering is intentional.

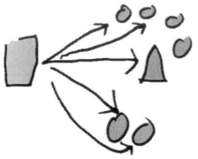

I constantly have signals go where they aren't supposed to. I feel many of the noises-clicks, whistles, whispers-and they are painful. I have to be careful, because I react very defensively to certain noises or touch. Parts of my body are untypically and abnormally sensitive with touch to the point that it is very agitating and even painful. I have trouble with motion.

Some of these complications are constant (like my agitation by specific touch or noise) and some of them are not. Those that are not constant can be caused by fatigue, sugar crash, socially overwhelmed, little brothers, and other agitators.

In short: I feel what I hear. When I am touched on the arm, I feel it in my leg. Snapping fingers affects my motor skills and can make me fall.

Likewise, because I don't develop filtered signals the same way, I don't always develop new "responses" to sensory information. Where a non-autistic person will "feel" a hand they see get hit that is not their own, an autistic person may not, because there is no directed signal to the brains saying "a hand was hit." like with many of the things in this book, this isn't universal. Each autistic individual processes signals uniquely. Some may "over sensitize" things they see happening to a separate individual.

Linear Thinking

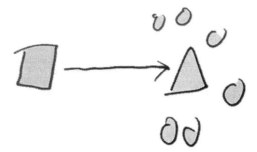

People who have good filters can function within a concept, like math. The filter focuses the brain on the subject at hand. When a neuro-typical individual talks about math, their thought process stays on the subject of math.

In short: if we are talking about math, we talk about math.

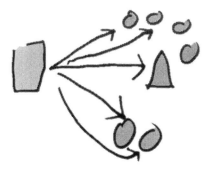

I consistently deviate from a defined domain when discussing a concept. While discussing math, I may start tying in music, science, religion, Saturday morning cartoons, etc. I "see" everything in my head as on a matrix, and when I am having a discussion, everything on that matrix is accessible. There is no wall or divider saying "you can't go there." Now part of my defense system has created some barriers—they aren't the "I understand why I can't go there," but more of the "I don't want to get hurt again by going there."

In short: if we are talking about math, I talk about liver transplants and the difference between Metallica bass players.

Propriety: Sacred vs Common

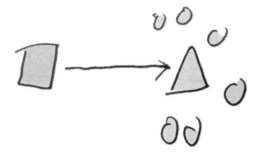

If a neuro-typical individual is functioning within an environment that requires propriety, they can filter out those things they view as improper. When in a professional setting, they can act professional. When in a religious setting, they can function accordingly. The formal, the proper, the sacred, the serious, and the dignified are all boundaries that a healthy filtering system comes to understand and implement.

In short: if we are at work, we use "work language". When we are at church, we use "church language". When we are at a social, we use "social language". Language is filtered based on our environment.

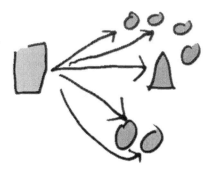

The concept of propriety can be a struggle for me: I understand what I understand, and I function like I function. Filtering out elements to contain parts of me while restraining other parts is very difficult and exhausting, if and when it can be done. I am the same regardless of the environment I am in.

For example: in college, I had a professor ask me why, in the middle of a paper about information systems, I was included discussions about Sigmund the Sea monster. In my head, it made sense. To him, it was an obscure and improper subject to include in a "proper paper."

I struggle with the line between "offensive words" and socially acceptable words. To me, "offensive" means I am attacking someone, and if I am not intentionally attacking someone, it is hard to understand how what I say is "offensive."

Instead, I have categorize words into "hurt words" and "words that help". I understand trying to be safe and avoid conflict and not wanting to hurt people, so I categorize words that way. In my head, words are words, and they all fly freely. But I work very hard at making sure I very deliberately pick which ones I use: I try to pick words I know will build up and avoid those I believe tear people down.

ROUTINE

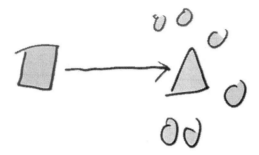

Routines are important to everyone. The nice thing about filters is that it allows individuals to produce multi-dimensional views of certain environments or routines.

For example: if a neuro-typical individual sits in the same chair every day in school/church/dinner, and a non-autistic person needs to change seats, that's usually fine (unless they have a very specific reason for wanting that chair). It's typically a simple matter to switch for whatever reason: a broken chair, a visitor, etc. The filters allow a repositioning of the items and persons in the room.

Filters work with routines to allow non-autistic people to step away from a routine if they need to.

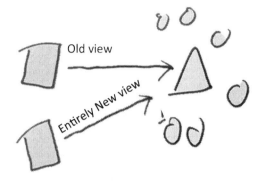

Repositioning myself is difficult. I have to construct a whole new "static view" of the environment or routine.

If that routine or environment is altered—like I have to sit in a different seat—I literally have to rebuild the entire view from scratch. The safe space or routine that was in place which allowed me to feel non-threatened has been altered. If a person feels threatened, the process they go through to reposition themselves and adjust may become very erratic, because the filters to create boundaries are not there. I have to rebuild the picture. I have to rebuild the routine.

Sensitive topic alert!

UNDERSTANDING IDENTITY & PREFERENCES

Now going along with my "not afraid to tread on sensitive topics," I wanted to discuss "Identity".

People with filters typically understand "I am a(n) __A__ so therefore I typically prefer __B__". Or "I am a(n) __A__ so there for I typically behave like __B__".

Without filters, both A and B can be called into question.

Identity [A] has to do with everything from our gender, to our nationality, to our culture, to the niche we associate ourselves with, to our job, and so on. Some of these we inherit from our parents, some we develop through our experiences and some are supposedly part of our programming.

As for preferences [B], there are socially imposed stereotypes, proprieties, preferences, and generally accepted rules of engagement that people with filters will typically subscribe to. Without those filters, all of these connections and parameters can become "vague". Yes, our environment and our chemical make-up may still encourage us in following a specific path. But psychologically, there is less of a defined construct.

To note: almost all humans can find their identity/preferences deviating and changing due to the natural human defense system. This defense system can be activated by injury, illness, psychological issues, and a plethora of other stimuli. But, because the autistic individual does not have filters to control or direct, or regulate the relocation of preferences, the outcome under these same scenarios will have greater variance.

Along this line: simply having an identity or preference that deviates from the generally accepted social construct is not the same as being autistic. There are dozens/millions of things that go into influencing our identity/preferences (society, defense system, experiences, genetics, ideology...). Autism simply adds a variable in it.

⚠️ Sensitive topic alert!

UNDERSTANDING ABSTRACT CONCEPTS

Not to be preachy, but continuing on the "not afraid to tread on sensitive topics": On the religious side, this has affected me as well. Holding onto "doctrines and creeds" is not that easy for me. I know them and catalogue them. I have studied a LOT of religions—the whole 200 section of the Huey, Dewey, AND Louie Decimal System. I might know a lot about them, but adhering to them is another thing.

Instead, I look at it from a rational approach: do I know if God is real? Do I believe Jesus is real? Is there evidence Jesus dies and rose again? If those are things that have happened, then I can have a foundation outside of dogma. And the rule is simple and right up my view point: Jesus reconciles us to God, and we are to love people and help them. So I can take my religious view without having to embrace a lot of filter-ish things like propriety, rules, affirmations, etc. I can approach it systematically.

I can ask the same for a lot of the other prophets, but, in the case of Christ, his death and resurrection are tangible events that have a claim and merit associated with it, so I can argue with it: If he died and rose again, we are reconciled with God. If not, then his words were simply nice words.

In short, regarding metaphysical realities: dogmas and creeds may be amusing—I might even be able to recite them—but intrinsically I hold on to concrete things I have reason to believe are real.

Again, I am not trying to preach. These are just my views and how I came about them. I realize other people will have different conclusions and validate information differently.

> So if either of these "Sensitive topic alerts" throw you off, make you uneasy or offended, or make you question your existence, welcome to the world of Autism. Your boxes amuse us.

Mental Shortcuts

In a typical brain function, the filters allow an individual to develop short cuts: when a person sees A, they automatically correspond it with B. If a person says one thing, the brain automatically jumps to a conclusion based on the short cuts. This is found in a lot of innuendo and social cues: The brain knows where a clue leads to. It also helps in deriving routines for simple tasks like making sandwiches or picking places to eat.

I do not have mental short cuts. Every time a question is asked, the brain goes through the same process each time, with many of the processes being dragged through a pond of information. Sometimes "simple questions" become overwhelming. While their neuro-typical counter-parts are using short cuts all over the place, I am having to go through each step, over and over again.

I have panicked making a peanut butter sandwich. When my wife asks where I want to go eat, all I see is a vision of a million stores, and they aren't even all restaurants or in the same State. I don't know what restaurants are on what road, so everything mushes together. When one restaurant makes it into the "long term memory" and/or routine, it will quickly become a favorite, because it means I am not stressing over trying to pull a visual out of the pond.

UNDERSTANDING THE IMPLIED

Neuro-filters have the ability to interpret things implied. In the illustration, the individual says "Swiss cheese is O.K." Someone who knows the individual will understand they are probably desiring something else. Even though someone may not know the individual, they still could probably read into the conversation that Swiss may not be the best option.

Someone like me without those filters will hear, "Swiss is an acceptable option" as "they want Swiss". There is no filter to illuminate any hidden nuances. *When* I learn that "acceptable" means "they want something else," the alternative can be anything - asparagus, steak, falafel, treadmill - since I have no filter to limit the options to cheese.

Typing "Swiss" so many times makes it a weird word... "Swiss, Swiss, Swiss, Swiss, Swiss, Swiss, Swiss, Swiss, Swiss, Swiss"

Understanding Facial Expressions

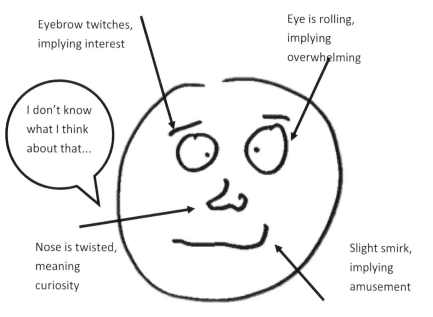

The filters in the neuro-typical design reads nuances in face and body movements. Words are only part of the conversation. The facial expressions allow the other person to read emotions and intent, such as "I'm annoyed", "I'm done", "conversation is over", "I have a crush", "I am not interested", "I am uncomfortable", "You have a blemish on your face" and so on.

I cannot read all the intents of the individual I am speaking to. Because of it, I have a long history of transgressing "the conversation should have been over a while ago", "the topic is making me uncomfortable" and "You really are annoying me and wish you would go away."

Understanding Time

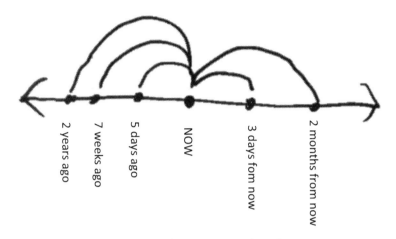

Filters allow individuals to organize abstract concepts like time. Filters allow individuals to quantify time: 2 days ago, 3 months from now...

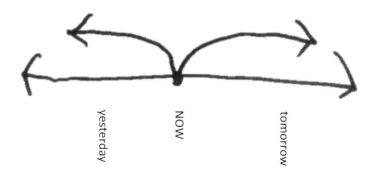

Without filters, time is vague. For people like me, there is yesterday, tomorrow, and now. If I am told something is happening in 3 months, my head thinks it is tomorrow.

There are phenomena where a person intrinsically processes every date. This is also part of the "absence of filter". The brain's filtering system will pick which days to remember and which to forget. Remembering all of them—like the absence of shortcuts—comes because the brain cannot determine which steps/days to filter out in a given process.

UNDERSTANDING FRIENDSHIP

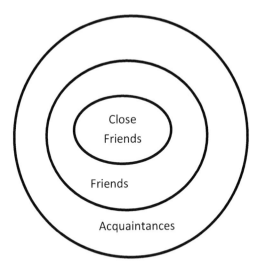

Filters allow the division between "Close Friends", "Friends", and "Acquaintances."

Not my friends

Without those filters, there is no line between "Sort of friends" and "Best friends". Mixed with the issue of understanding boundaries, a lot of lines are crossed.

This has been a hard one for me to work with my son over, because I transgressed so many lines. I am in my 50s now, and I have very few people I call my friend, and the only reason I do is because they reach out to me. Other than that, I don't really understand what a friend is. I honestly do not know how to tell.

Answering the Question

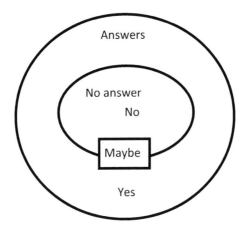

Filters allow the user to organize decision making, dividing up answers and non-answers. With those filters, it is easier to deduce "Yes", and "No", and it also opens the opportunity to "Maybe".

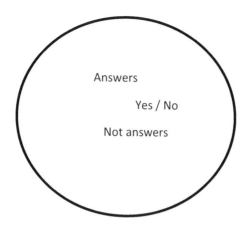

Without those filters, the line between answers/non-answers and yes/no become vague. On top of that, "Maybe" is ambiguous at best. Many people like me see "Maybe" as "yes".

Sometimes, an individual like me "set in their way" because having a safe "Yes" and a safe "Answer" prevents them from having to wander back into the indecisive zone. An example of this would be any routine:

What would you like to eat?
    The same thing.

Where would you like to sit?
    The same place

Do you want to wear this cotton blend like you did yesterday and the day before and the day before?
    Yes

Meltdown vs Temper Tantrum

Temper tantrums are emotionally stimulated forms of manipulating the responsible parties. They are rarely thrown in solitude.

Meltdowns are electrical overloads caused by too many signals. Again, the overload and misdirected signals caused by poor filtering. Those signals can come instantaneously, or they can build up over a period of time. Meltdowns don't care if anyone is watching. The individual just wants to reset. Up until they reset, they can be iirational, because external stimuli are irrelevant.

One of the most important things is to realize a meltdown is not from bad parenting. It is not because the child is bad or trying to manipulate. It is an internal defense reaction from becoming overloaded.

It is also important to understand that, without learning healthy coping mechanisms, meltdowns will evolve into shutdowns and "short tempers" as the child grows into adulthood. Although the "meltdown" can be unavoidable, the individual needs to understand the consequences of their responses. The social environment has the right to defend itself just as much as the individual, and if we allow our response to violate the safety of the social environment, there will be consequences. So it is critical for the individual to understand how they function and the healthiest means to manage their overloads.

There are table comparisons all over the internet. I will just post a few differences. This is not an exhaustive comparison by any means

TEMPER TANTRUM	MELTDOWN
Goal oriented (They want something)	No goal
Watching/desiring reactions and responses	Not interested in reaction or responses… it only makes it worse
Will avoid negative response	Doesn't care about response and can even be personally detrimental
Ends quickly when goal is obtained	Takes time to reset
Individual is in control—is using temper to obtain goal	Is not in control—in absolute defense mode
Will communicate source of temper tantrum	Will ramble and verbally attack irrationally
Are deliberate	Are not deliberate
Will increase to obtain goal	Wants to find resolution and restoration
Temper tantrums can actually evolve into meltdowns (they get so worked up they overload themselves)	Meltdowns can never lead into temper tantrums

In short, its about intent. If there is a goal to their behavior, and the behavior stops when they obtain the goal, it is probably a temper tantrum. If there is no rational goal and the person does not respond to external stimuli, if you can threaten to spank them, take away their toys, burn the house down… it is a meltdown.

In many ways, a meltdown and a panic attack look very similar.

Emotions

There are many other complications that any given autistic individual will experience. We are all different simply because we are human, and the points of deviation in the filtering are different for every individual.

Other complications I have are in the scope of emotions: I can't understand or process things like embarrassment well. If I see it on the TV, I have to leave the room, even if I know it is situational comedy. I do not rationally process guilt or jealousy, and intentionally lying is very difficult for me. On the flip side, I also want to be safe and avoid feeling bad, so I will say almost anything without regard to if it is true or not—I just want to be safe and I want whatever is threatening me to go away or stop. I don't even ask myself if it is true or not. I just want to be safe.

In short, I cannot read your face, your body motions, your intent, your hidden content in your words, your emotions and feelings, etc. My wife, whom I love with all my being, hated me for years when we first met, and I had no idea. I ran over her toes constantly. Good thing I didn't know, or I would have left her alone.

Understanding Labels & Medicine

Most medicines used in trying to assist autistic people in coping are addressing our filtering system (or lack there of).

Stimulants are being used to "encourage" whatever filters we have available to work or work harder, thus helping control where the signals go.

Depressants are trying to decrease the amount of signals being sent.

It has been asked if it is better to not "label" a person as autistic. Let me be frank: Autistic people know they are different, and they know they are having trouble with the world around them. Hiding from them the reason why and preventing them from obtaining the skills that would enable them to not only function but also thrive with their unique design is cruel.

I struggled for decades to understand who I was. As I have mentioned, I have a trail of train wrecks behind me. I have friends who "probably" fall on the spectrum who wrecked their lives as well, trying to self-medicate, fix things, escape, and so on.

Will people "abuse" and "try to get by with things" if they have a label? Of course they will. Anyone who has something unique about themselves will try to see where and how they can use it as an advantage. That's also a part of growing up and developing an identity. Robbing them of that opportunity to understand who they are will not stop them from trying to fix things.

So, where do we go from here?

I think the most important thing is to understand that people on the spectrum take time to process things that non-autistic individuals find simple. People like me experiment to find boundaries that people with filters take for granted. People like me WILL push past what others consider acceptable to understand where the boundaries are. Where non-autistic people process things through a systematic methodology, people like me are pulling information from a pool.

Please don't view us as rebels, trouble makers, sinners, deviants or social stains. Understand that the things people with filters take for granted are not as cut and dry for us. Forgive us when we find it hard to change, can't bend to community demands, or have issues subscribing to social norms. Lines are blurry, and how we fit in is confusing. Be patient when we try to control the environment because various stimuli and environmental variables create various complications for us, complications that are masked or subliminal to non-autistic people.

In the end, I have adapted a very simple, 2 step outlook:

> **Takiwātanga**: it is the Maori word for autism, derived from the Maori phrase "tōku/tōna anō takiwā". it means "my/his/her own time and space". Give people time to grow, give people time to change. Give people time to learn who they are.
>
> **Galatians 6:2**. It simply says "Carry each other's burdens, and in this way fulfill the Law of Christ." Because I understand Jesus reconciled me to God, I understand my call is to help others, to help others carry their burdens. One of the old English words for the Love of God (Agape) seen in older English lit is "charity", because

the Love of God was considered an action verb, not simply a feeling verb. In 1 Corinthians 12:12-27, Paul writes that we are members of one body, and no member is greater or lesser than the other: the foot does not say to the eye "you are not a foot, so we do not need you." No matter how hard it is to see at times, every person has a place, every person has a purpose, every person is important. You are important.

So, that's what I have. I know not everyone will agree with everything I wrote. That is o.k. If you have met one autistic person, then you have met one autistic person. That is one of the things that makes being human so special. We are all different. God literally put it in the design. I hope you all have a great life. Till next time.

Zarqnon the Embarrassed

Takiwatanga

Galatians 6:2

Appendix:

This is an old PowerPoint diagram I developed years ago to explain the difference between how those on the spectrum might see something vs someone not on the spectrum

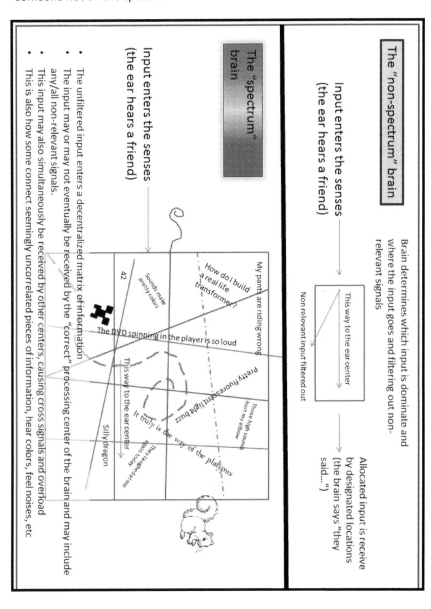

Made in the USA
San Bernardino, CA
07 January 2020